Yellow

chemopoetry from a caretaker's journey

Chad Michael Rimmer

Cover Photo by Chad Michael Rimmer

ISBN: 1983865923
ISBN-13: 978-1983865923

For Natalie

Contents

Introduction i
Africa Lost 2
The Diagnosis 4
Post Diagnosis 7
Truth 8
Matins 10
Compline 12
Dr. Data 15
Blood and Water 16
Poison and Prayer 18
Little Death 20
Who are you? 21
Strong 22
Fragrance 26
Lament for Eve 28
Hannah's Song 30
Love your Enemy 32
Grace 35
Anesthesia 36
The Hawk 38
Holy other, Wholly other 40
Too deep for words 42
Healing 43
Yellow 44
Rhythm of Life 46
Good Morning Sonnet 47

Firefly 48
While you were home healing 50
Always the mountain 51
Good News 54
The sign...57
Socks and Sliced Bread 58
Radiation 60
The Monarch 62
The proper art of Healing 64
She walks..67
Ta beauté 70
Hard to be light hearted 71
The return to Hann Mariste 72
Bluebird 74
A Star in the West..76
Being or Becoming? 77
There will be Love..80
Sandalwood 84
What the child knows..85
Twister 90
Yaangi fi..95
Twelfth Night 98
Dust..100
I Miss Me 104
On Beauty...106
Logos..115

INTRODUCTION

To be a poet is to be a creator.

During my family's blessed years of living in bonnie Scotland, an elder Scottish priest once told me that the old Scots word for a Poet was *Makr*, or maker. Plato and Aristotle taught that the task of a Poet is to make something. But unlike woodworkers or manufacturers or civil engineers, the Poet does not use technical skill to make something built for a purpose. The Poet uses words to make sense of the experience of life in the fluidity of real time.

Perhaps in this way poetry is unlike any other creative task. Even novelists craft a complete story, *fait accompli*. Like an architect who constructs a finished functional structure according to their intended design, an author narrates the reader towards an end for which the story was made. In this way, prose is propositional. It proposes a fully formed story to the reader. (This is why the art of writing fictional, philosophical, theological, scientific or journalistic prose is…well…prosaic.) But poetry is different.

Poetry invites the reader to witness the Poet's moment of wonder as they try to understand that which they behold. In this sense, poetry doesn't intend to actually make any***thing*** – poetry is the act of making. A poem is not created. A poem is the written record of a moment of creativity. Ultimately, a poem is an invitation for the reader to participate in that creative process of making meaning; to be present as the Poet tries to transform their perception into knowing.

That poetic process of meaning-making demands attention. Making sense out of our being-in-the-world requires that we focus our perception at some depth. Knowing is the result of a peculiar kind of seeing. The seventeenth century Anglican priest and poet Thomas Traherne called it the 'Infant-eye'. He once wrote, 'Covet a lively sense of all you know, of the Excellency of God, and of Eternal Love; of your own Excellency, and of the worth and value of all Objects whatsoever. For to feel is as necessary as to see their Glory.'

Spiritual sight happens when our soul is quiet enough to feel what is seen and unseen; when we are still enough to hear what is said and unsaid. The whole world is constantly communicating by its being. A 'lively sense' feels the whole spectrum of that communication between ourselves, the objects in our natural or built environment, and the creatures that we encounter in our daily experience. Cultivating a depth of holy listening opens us to the possibility of sensing the true significance of any given situation, even those that seem mundane. When we are blessed to see the holiness that fills everything with meaning…that is a poetic moment.

I have been a student of poetry for a long time. I love the deep resonance that happens when you are invited to feel what someone else sees. I have also written poetry for some time in order to discover how I see the world; or maybe to understand how I feel about the world. Every discipline helps us make sense of our experience of life in a different way. As a biologist, I know that inductive knowledge of how the world works helps us steward, heal, restore and conserve life. As a theologian I know that systematic theology is a way to frame our faith for others. As a pastor I know that spiritual practices nurture deep solidarity. As an ethicist I know that moral reasoning in community helps us develop a critical consciousness about how we ought to live out shared values. And as a poet, I know that poetry helps us understand a truth that can only be sensed when we are attentive to the phenomenal and ephemeral flux of life in real time and space.

Through poetry, I participate in the ancient practice of contemplation that has inspired and confounded philosophers, artists and theologians in the eternal search for truth, goodness and beauty.

Throughout my years of international and multicultural work I have been writing poems as a means of theological and philosophical reflection. Each poem is a little essay, an attempt to make sense of the kind of illumination that breaks into events that seem uniquely difficult or graced. In order to help others learn to watch for these moments of in-breaking, I have from time to time shared poems in my teaching. But this book is the first attempt to share some of my poems publicly. The impetus for my desire to share these poems from this particular year in my life is as simple as it is sublime. My wife was diagnosed with cancer.

This arresting reality broke into the flow of my life, and its entry was not clean. Cancer shattered our life into pieces that were flung so far and so fast, we weren't sure we could put it back together. In order to seek specialized treatment in America, we were forced to evacuate our life in Senegal, West Africa and indefinitely postpone our life's work. We had to leave a faithful circle of friends and loved ones and move our children to a different continent with a different culture and language. We had to leave our symbol-sanctified-stuff behind in a home that we weren't sure we would ever see again. Suddenly and brutally, we lost the spatial and temporal touchstones that helped us make sense of life. We had to give up long standing family traditions and rituals in order to adapt our life to someone else's rhythms. My wife and I have always cultivated intentional liturgical rituals of spirituality, celebration, health, and wholeness with our children. But suddenly we had to glean hurried moments from the time and space left over in someone's house or the corners of a cancer clinic. As is the case with displaced people who are forced to migrate from their meaning-rich home, cancer physically forced us to become strangers in a strange land. We had to learn to see, interpret and follow new signposts towards an uncertain destination. We felt the disorientation that gave rise to the ancient Hebrew poet's lament as they sat down by the waters of Babylon and wept when they remembered the life they left behind in Zion. Their cry was not nostalgia for a time gone by. It was the exilic cry of confusion for having lost the natural, cultural, religious and linguistic ecology in which their life made sense. We shared their poetic yearning to make sense out of a whole new world. For my family, being forced into a medical exile altered our world in an instant.

In one half hour meeting with my wife's oncologist, our life's goals seemed to painfully contract to a single search. All I wanted to know was the path toward healing. Of course in the long struggle against sarcoma, life is filled with all sorts of knowledge about best practices and oncological research. But healing is an art, and no medical protocol is sufficient. There is much more to the process of healing. It will not be found by looking to one side of a spirit/body duality. In order to completely heal, we have to remember our full identity as a human creature. That is hard to do when you are trying to make sense of a displaced life while suffering the vertigo of cancer and treatments. Like the Hebrew poet in exile, almost everything that you recognize about your life recedes into a memory that is simply no longer sensible. To make sense of it all, you must experience your new world as if for the first time – as a child perceives. So this became my poetic task.

But I must be clear - the direct experience of having cancer is not something that I can know, because this disease is not mine to bear. That burden fell to my wife, and most of the time I honor the sublimity of her experience with respectful silence. My poetic task was not to make sense of the experience of having cancer, rather the experience of caring for my beloved who has cancer.

Anyone who has intimately cared for a loved one over an extended period of time knows that caring demands an attentive quietness. It demands a certain sense of timing that responds to things unsaid, learns to interpret groans too deep for words and anticipates quiet moments of joy, which become milestones that will go unnoticed by others who do not stay present or quiet long enough to even notice the significance of the simple. Caring is poetic in that the caretaker must practice a spiritual seeing that tries to feel the needs, emotions, hope, struggle, truth, goodness and beauty of life in its fullness, which includes deep suffering alongside deep grace. The need to listen deeply to medical personnel, my children, myself and ultimately my wife aligned with my inner need to write poetry. And through that poetic process I began to make sense of her journey toward healing.

Now, please allow a brief word about the poems. As I mentioned above, these poems are an invitation for you to witness moments of meaning-making as I experienced them. They are presented in a basic chronological order from our evacuation through her diagnosis, surgery, radiation, chemotherapy, and our new life of living with cancer. They are interspersed with seemingly random but always meaningful events that give life texture and feeling. Some of the poems were written at the Sarcoma Clinic of Duke University Cancer Center and Hospital in the caring company of nurses, PAs, chaplains, doctors, technicians, staff, environmental services personnel and therapists to whom I owe gratitude that can never be fully expressed. Some of the poems were written while she was quietly healing in a home.

Some of them were written while we convalesced in nature. All of them were written somewhere along our family's mysterious and wonder-filled journey towards healing. Living with cancer is an experience marked by profound change, disorientation, uncertainty, loss, recovery, discovery, confirmation, limits, breakthroughs, ecstasy, fear, joy, anger, peace, pain, pleasure, sublimity, silliness and everything in between. As such, these poems are asymmetrical, sometimes raw, sometimes beautiful, but always honest. They are written in many different styles – sometimes sonnets of various forms, sometimes terza rima, sometimes simple rhyme, sometimes haiku, sometimes metered and sometimes free verse. Some reflect my unique experience, and some are written in dialogue with the thoughts of others.

This dialogue is done in the spirit of accompaniment. Just as I accompanied my wife and my children through this experience of healing, I was helped along by the meaning-making witness of people of good will that have walked this way before me. I find fellow pilgrims in the work of philosophers, theologians, poets, mystics, Holy Scriptures, musicians, artists, and all sorts of non-human creatures that communicate truth about nature's will-to-life. As inter-subjective beings, we are always formed in relationships. My relationship with these fellow sojourners through prayer, reading and deep listening helped me transform this pilgrimage of healing into a process of meaning making.

So I share these poems not as mere intellectual or emotional exhibitionism, but in the hope that you, too, might be aided by joining in the dialogue. Whether you have cancer, are caring for someone living with cancer, or whether you are just interested in the poetry, I pray that witnessing my generative moments helps you cultivate an awareness of your own process of meaning making. But ultimately, I am sharing this collection of poetry to honor my wife, whose own blessed will-to-life throughout this traumatic journey with Ewing's Sarcoma is the embodiment of grace that inspired me to listen and to feel, which in the end became, as Traherne said, a way to understand my own nature.

By cultivating a lively sense of all that is to be known in this experience, I have been blessed by my wife. I have been blessed to see her grace and beauty in action. Her path to healing has not been a combat against fear. Rather, her way of healing is a testament to the true power of creaturely meekness and the ultimate nature of the Creator's enduring love. These poems are my tribute to her, in honor of her healing. In publishing them I am inviting you into my many moments of wonder as I was engaged in the task of understanding that which I beheld; the task of turning my perception into knowing; the creative task of making sense out of our journey through scans, surgeries, radiation, and chemotherapy. In a word it is, ***chemopoetry***. Through each poem, I pray that you sense something of our search for healing in partnership with the Divine. And I hope these poems help you feel a lively sense of yours.

Please excuse me, for this whole introduction has been very prosaic. So onto the poetry. And may you be well.

Peace to you,
Chad

YELLOW

chemopoetry from a caretaker's journey

Africa Lost

Sure the beating drums are sounding
as pestles on the mortise wood,
as waves upon the painted pirogues,
and the rattle of palmieres.

Life first sounded from this cradle
in Africa's fertile valleys.
For me, it took a whole lifetime
to find this source and drink deeply.

We dug our toes deep in her sands.
We wrapped our hearts in her tissues,
yellows and reds and greens so rich.
Black and white are woven.

Resting soft in Maman's breast,
it seemed the Odyssey was through.
We found our love, life and beauty
thriving in Sophia's garden.

But just as quick as we had come
the whirring of a broken wing
lifts us out of our paradise,
exiles us to another shore.

From here, I cannot hear her drums,
the millet grinding, her fishing boats,
her sweet songs of dawning prayers,
or dance to her gracious, soulful time.

And as we rise from her embrace,
in the blackness of this cold night,
I dare not speak what's in my heart.
I wonder if Africa's lost.

Is my flight into this midnight
the mystic darkness that I fear
of having seen the plenitude
only to have it veiled again?

Like Julian who held the cosmos,
and in ecstasy shed her tears,
then blinked to wipe them all away,
and was left with a hazelnut.

Did Francis, Bernard, Catherine,
Teresa or Hildegard feel
light from beyond themselves again?
Or did they learn to love shadows?

Can I live long east of Eden
knowing the fruit that lies within,
knowing my exile was not caused
but by the nature of nature?

I ache to feel that *theosis*
of living so close to the land
in the thin place where we were born,
to walk as Enoch in the light.

But, perhaps I have not lost her.
She flees with me in the darkness.
I can't see through the veil yet,
but I hear her drums beat for me.

The Diagnosis

(or *Sheol*)

Where am I now?
I'm sitting in this place.
The sign on the wall says "Consultation Room".
He came to me,
The sterile smell of anti-life on his tired hands.
He spoke a word for me,
"Malignant".
There were other words that I heard,
But did not feel like this one,
"Cancer".
Strange,
The word that he spoke did not create.
It ricocheted off the walls, off my ears,
And returned to me,
Empty.
He left me.
And in that place I sat alone, wondering,
Where am I now?
This is no place, just a space.
Empty.

The Psalmist called this place Sheol.
It's the empty place.
The low place.
The uncreated place.
The space where the word did not create
Either weal or woe.

Some say it's hell, but it's not.
It's Sheol.
The place where the word cannot create.

Cancer.
Some have said that this word creates fear,
Or dread,
Sadness or anger,
Or chaos or despair.
But the diagnosis is strange.
It confirmed,
It revealed,
It projected,
It described,
It delineated a new space,
But then it returned empty.
And now I sit here in it, alone.

Where am I?
Some say it's hell, but it's not.
It's empty.
Sheol.
Strange.
I am not afraid, for it did not create fear.
I am not sad, for it cannot unmake you.
This is no hell,
For that word which he spoke
Cannot make a suffering place,
Ultimately it cannot make at all.

So I will not despair,
Because hope will fill this empty place.

I will return to her,
And listen to her breathe,
And wait to hear Your Word
That will not return empty.
The Word that will stay with us
and make this space bloom into a healing place.

Post Diagnosis

Just after the flood
We loosed the Dove to seek hope.
She sang, "Follow me."

Truth

"Okay," you said, when the verdict came.
For my beloved I was forced to be a dreaded Angel.
I brought the message,
from his mouth to your ears,
I carried the news faithful and clear,
I spoke the Truth that we all feared.
The Truth about where we are,
What it is,
Where we must go,
And what we must leave behind.

"Okay," you said,
As if you had long before turned your face toward this Truth.
And perhaps you had welcomed it already.
Somewhere in your heart,
Knowing pain had a purpose.
Knowing the Truth that our bodies know
    long before our minds.
Knowing that you knew the Truth
        long before I spoke it.

What is the Truth?
    Pilate once asked the man from Nazareth.
What is the Truth that we so dread?
Was it really of cells and rates and results?
Or was it a knowing far more real?
A Truth about who He is and what we are?
We knew the Truth already,

Because Thomas told me four centuries ago,
God made us more by making us less.
The Truth has never been more clear
that our minds don't have to clearly know the Truth,
because we are not mere rationality.
We are no Angels,
and like you said, that is "Okay".
Because while they know, they do not feel.
No pain, sure. No suffering.
But then no touch, no compassion, no joy,
of their own or of yours.
They were at the tomb,
But did they feel the pain of nails or the rush of new life?
Then do they Truly know of what they speak?

Well I do.
I know the Truth because when I speak it, it hurts.
Because it is a Truth about your pain and I cry.
Because your suffering unleashes my compassion,
Because my fear reveals our joy
in what could have been lost.
Yes, it is "okay" that we know the Truth.
And you already knew.
There is no dread in it,
For in its dark shadow the light of our joy can shine.
So, my beloved,
I am no dreaded Angel.
I am much less, and so are you.
And, once spoken,
that Truth has set us free.

Matins

O Lord, open my lips,
And my mouth shall proclaim your praise.
Sometimes by the rush of the wild Linville gorge,
Sometimes by the clarion call of the priest bird,
calling forth life from the Amazonian artery.
Sometimes by the nightingale,
alit upon the heights of the Danish Cedar,
trying to catch the first rays of your light
that pour over the rim of morning.
Sometimes by the bleat of the Highland sheep
across a heather rimmed loch.
Sometimes by the din of children,
stirring in the townships of the Cape,
Sometimes by the crashing pulse of the Atlantic,
Sometimes by the call to prayer,
over the sands of the Sahel.
Sometimes by the moan of a camel in the Negev,
outside the Bedouin's cave.
Even one time by the bells of the Holy Sepulcher,
declaring new life at dawn from the tomb on that Holy Mount.
Life, open our lips, and the world shall proclaim your praise.

But this morning light creeps through the blinded portal.
The sounds of today's resurrection are a clicking pump,
the beep of a call button,
the white whir of a hydraulic bed.
And I wonder, can this fabricated symphony proclaim your praise?

Is this as it was in the beginning, and as it shall be forever,
 amen?
This is not the poetry of creatures,
 bearing witness
 in the morning of their being.
No, this is the artifice of controlled healing
 in plastic, aluminum and toxic sterility.
This is a protocol that can proclaim the death of what you
 fear…
But can it proclaim life?
Can it proclaim joy come the morning?
I decide no, and settle back into my sorrow that spent the
night.

And then I hear it.
Matins.
By the rustle of a bed sheet,
By the rasp of your dry throat,
By the deep pull of your breath,
By the blue of your windows opening your soul to the wind,
 to the breath,
 to the energy,
 to the fire that proclaims life to the fear,
 to the nausea,
 to the fatigue,
 to the night.
Glory to the Spirit, the Giver of Life.
For in you, my icon of hope, strength, renewal, and beauty,
I see as it was in the beginning,
And how it shall be forever. Amen.

Compline

You lie each night,
A repose at the end of love, life, laugh, loss.
Fatiguée, je suis.
Still waiting for the healing.
Knowing this is healing.
Smiling under sad eyes,
You lament what you yearn for.
The time to whisper ancient words,
Needing them to be spoken,
Yearning for them to be spoken,
Hating that they are spoken for you.

So I come.
Needing to speak them for you.
Yearning to speak them for you.
Hating that I speak them for you.
Thankful that I can speak them for you.

My hand to your heart,
Palm to breast,
My hand to your hurt,
Palm to wound.
We breathe.
I can't touch it, but my heat finds it there.
We breathe.
The universe breathes.
Grounding, opening, receiving, waiting.
We breathe.

She comes,

Entering, filling, seeking, searching.

She breathes in you.

She who moved over the void,

She who separated,

She who inspired,

She who created,

She who revived,

She who resurrected,

She who animated,

She breathes in you.

She searches,

She finds,

She enlightens,

She holds,

She heals,

She protects,

She abides.

We breathe.

We feel her in the space between palm and breast.

We feel her in the space between palm and wound.

We trust she is there.

We know she heals.

We know she hears the ancient words.

Send your holy angels to attend,

In the darkness where my hand can't find your hurt,

When my hand can't warm your heart.

Let them abide.

Guide your waking.
Guard your sleeping.
That awake you may watch with Christ,
And asleep you may rest in peace.
The peace of knowing
That when we are tired
She neither slumbers nor sleeps.
And in Her peaceful presence,
You find the grace of sleep.

Your compline is spoken.

But mine has just begun.
Because She is here I cannot sleep.
There is no rest from my watch.
Because She is here, I turn my palms to Her now.
There is no one to speak the ancient words for me.
Perhaps David or Jeremiah or Martha.
But She is here, so I want to watch.
I want to wait.
I want to feel.
I want to know She abides.
Her breath to your heart,
Her breath to your hurt,
Searching, holding, healing.
And now I hear it,
This is my compline.
To know you rest in Her.

Dr. Data

We sat in the room.
You stood.
We were talking about her life,
Not yours.
We asked, "Is it enough?"
You said, "Trust what the data suggests."
Well, let me ask you, Dr. Data,
How many salamanders have you seen?
A dozen you say?
And how many red salamanders have you seen?
None, you say?
So, it seems the data suggests red salamanders don't exist.
But, my sister, I've seen a red salamander.
You see, the data suggests that
my beloved should not be sitting here asking this question.
And yet, here she is,
struggling to wrap her heart around a decision.
So, Dr. Data, I ask you to remember,
We're talking about her life, not yours.
Now let us ask again…

Blood and Water

(Zephaniah 12:8-12, John 19:34, Luke 2:22-38)

The Seer gazed on the one that we pierced
and saw a great wave of compassion run.
It was the flow of a Holy Spirit

that covered those who lost their first born son.
A gracious release from supplications
of those in mourning for what they had done.

But did he see the same consolation
When we had sacrificed on the altar,
unjustly, the firstborn of creation?

Uncreated, yet born of a mother.
Mary wept when a spear pierced his bare side,
And our healing flowed as blood and water.

Would Zephaniah ease me if I cried,
like Mary, when they gave you bitter wine
to dull my love's flesh for to pierce your side?

This mix of blood and water is a sign,
of salvation's door revealed through your wound,
that healing can flow through the plastic line.

So now when my soul hurts as they pierce you,
like Mary, who knew that her soul would mourn,
the Seer's vision will console my view.

When the Queen of Creation's flesh is torn,
Anna, Simeon and I can now see,
Blood and water flow where new life is born.

Like birth and death, when their fusion is free,
Spirit can render renaissance holy.

Poison and Prayer

Deep in the forest we found the Place of Pain.
In the grove, a trunk once strong,
    is now compromised from within.
Now to restore the balance, they say,
    we must shake hands with the devil.
So I take my seat,
    and take my breath,
    and watch them divert the flow.
The pure canal, that river of life
    once carried nourishment.
But now it runs with a tide of something foreign.
As I sit in silence at your banks.
I listen to this current.
Bubbling down.
Pulsing in.
Changing your color,
Bleaching the firmament.
The vista around you is dressed in life,
    still images of blooms that will not sway
    because there is no breeze in this space.
The only movement is a rising chemical tide
    that brings prescribed death with each new poisonous wave.
And yet, in your garden,
    a shoot of hope much deeper than this saturation.
It grows from a place we'll never find,
Hidden in the matrix of life,
Woven into the fabric of you,
And covered now in the purple shawl of prayer.

With eyes closed, I am soothed by the radiant strength of its
defiant fragility.
And I smile, and rest tranquil.
Because I know you've found the Place of Peace.

Little Death

Schopenhauer told me every waking is a little life,
    And every sleep is a little death.
Some say, no, but I know it is so.
For when you fall,
I grieve a little.
I want to reach out
    And gently pull you back to sense,
    Or call out, "Talitha cumi!"
Because I don't want to miss
    A single moment of life with you.
But this desire is no agape,
it is my selfish yearning.
Because I know your soul aches for rest,
Your body calls out
For the way that makes for peace.
I can see it in the throb of your veins,
Expanding under the tension of welcoming a new force.
I can hear it in the broken cadence of your breath,
    Laboured by the exhaustion of healing.
So I quietly retreat to my vigil,
And let you die a little death.
Letting you go is my sacrifice of praise for healing.
Yet, though you leave,
    I am consoled in my grief.
Because I see that pulse of life
    That will bring you back to me.
And it's ambrosia to watch that light of new life,
Resurrect you at each new waking.

WHO ARE YOU?

Who are you?
Let me verify.
343665, Procedure?
36.8°?
D142526?
136 lbs.?
5/13/76?
10:15?
98%?
126/84?
0.3 WBC?
1000 ml over 2 hours?
9318?

Wait.
Take my hand.
Now I know.
You're my love.

Strong

Like Delilah, I shaved your head in secret.
Like Samson, you emerged from the night shorn.
    yet miraculously your power was intact.
Your power to break the chains of pain after each cycle
    and rise up under the weight of each test
    to topple pillars of uncertainty
    with some indefatigable energy.

Like Samson, there are those that watch you in awe,
    and yearning to confirm some myth of the human will,
        they pay pious homage to your rock-hard core,
        bow to a fierceness
          that spites the boatman
                though he already received an advance on the
                crossing,
        They worship a war they think you are waging.

But the secret of Samson was misunderstood.
He was confused from whence strength came,
        and they are, too.
Samson sought strength
        In the death of the death-dealer,
And in the end, the vengeance killed him.
Coming in hot destroyed him.
A rock hard core was his demise,
    not his strength.
And neither is it yours.

To see the source of Samson's strength,
They must not look to the Rock,
They must look to the stream beneath it.
En-hakkore empowered him.
"The Spring of the One who called him to life".
See the gentle source!
The cool, clear font of Life
Nourishes, and never annihilates.

Don't they know they must do the same to find yours?
They watch your shorn crown in awe of your enduring
strength.
But like Samson, they misunderstand the source.
It is more profound than they are willing to look,
More real than the rock they want to see.
You are no rock,
For your bones have been broken.
You are not fierce,
For you weep to know the tender touch of another day's
dawn.
You are no warrior,
For you pray peace to be restored to the rebellion in your
body.
You know, far more than they,
That warring only ever depletes.
As one familiar with suffering,
You dare not valorize violence in pursuit of hope.
Because yours is the Power perfected in weakness.

Yours is the strength of fragility
Refined in the knowledge of love that will topple temples of resolve
By breaking foundations of fear
With a gentle trickle of hope
That erodes the ramparts of hollow shibboleths
Destined to echo meaningless clichés about strength and power
By those who have never suffered want of anything
and reveals that bare truth about the gentleness of life
and the limits of human ability
that is known by all who have suffered the blessed resignation
in which the true power of Grace becomes known.

No, if they really want to see your strength,
They must not look to the rock that stands before them,
But the daisy which grows out from under it,
nurtured by the stream.
It will never seek to destroy the rock that looms above it.

It will simply,
Persistently,
Wonderfully,
Gently,
Kindly,
Justly,
Beautifully,
Peaceably
Grow.

Not lashing out tendrils to crush,
But sending its roots
    down,
        To places
        unseen,
    To drink
    deeply
Of the Spring
    of the One
        who calls
            her
                to
                 Life.

Fragrance

You are tired.
I am proud.
Your strength and grace I expect to see,
But none the less, seeing inspires awe.
Gratitude for your strength
That carries you to the point of sleep.
Renewal.

I draw the sheet and bend to kiss goodnight,
To breathe in the Spirit as I have for years,
To fill me with the fragrance of you.
You inspire a familiar perfume in my soul,
Like she who softened Solomon,
I know it is you standing in this theater of love
Because, even blinded,
I know the fragrance of your soul.
    A cluster of henna blossoms is your hope,
    A channel of nard, myrrh and frankincense is your love,
    Pomegranate and cinnamon are your joy,
    Aloes and saffron are your grace,
    Your breath like the orchard of apples.
I bend and breathe, expecting this familiar bouquet.

But who is this that I breathe?
As if embarrassed I open my eyes to see.
It is you. But something more?
I don't know this scent that arrested my kiss.
No saffron or cinnamon or henna or myrrh.
But neither is this the sweet, sharp smell of death.
No, I am too familiar with that pungent portent.

There is good news that it is nowhere to be found.
This is not the fragrance of death,
    but this is not the fragrance of your life.
So what?
This is the smell of toxic healing.
A strange way to protect the garden.
It is the soot of fire fighting fire.
A scorching that overwhelms the blooms
    And masks the nectars
    And floods the channels,
    For a season that lingers between hope and harvest.
But while the scent disorients me,
Four senses and faith tell me
I am in the same place I have always been.
I've just never been here during this season before.

So I welcome the fragrance of your fallowing into my soul.
And I give thanks that the wind of your strength
    and hope
    and love
Waft this new scent to me.

And now I know it is the aroma of patient preparation.
For in your garden, this fire is releasing new seeds
    And preparing a new seedbed, fresh and clean.
    Where soon, my love, your season of joy will bloom.
The spiced fragrance of your life will return.
With my eyes shut, I will breathe,
and know you have awoken from this healing sleep.
Then I will rejoice in your Spring.

Lament for Eve

(or *Lament for the Body)*

Since I have known you, you have been Eve.
Not to this Adam, but to the world.
The Ishshah, the life giver.
Not just for who we have made,
But in what we have become,
Wherefore we have thrived,
For whom we have welcomed.
Eve, the one who knows and nurtures,
Ishshah, the Life Giver.

And now comes the paradox,
For to heal her,
    The Life Giver must be made barren.
To prepare the field for new life, all must be razed.
And for this season, your vibrant landscape has changed.
Your crown can no longer hold the cascade that framed the
    visage of joy.
The banks of your icy blue pools are barren,
    stained dark with fatigue.
The font of your love and laughter is parched and pale.
The soft ridges that once comforted
    Are hardened and mined to access
    The sacred river of life that is now poisoned.
The gentle palms that once caressed
    Are now cracked from bearing the burden.

The warm canals are dry and painful.
The valley's fold that hid the soft mysterious shade
Are laid bare to the hot light.

On my pilgrimage I struggle to recognize
This once familiar way.
The ancient altars have been stripped,
Your landscape burned,
Your cairns laid plain.
Those who fight for life have scorched and scarred
the Life Giver.

But I know it must be so.
The stubble must be burned
to conserve and nurture the good soil
where the seed lies deep within,
Pulsing with life, not harmed by the war that wages around it.
At peace now, it rests, until Eve awakens from the dust.
I know Ishshah, and she will live.
Unlike Jeremiah, I don't care how long, O Lord.
Instead of wandering the ruins and lamenting the dust,
I will just sit at the gates of your garden,
And wait at the edge of your wadi
Until the river of life breaks its banks again,
And this desert blooms.

Hannah's Song

(or *Praise for the Body*)

Like Eli, I've sat with you in the temple,
While you wept and prayed.
Like Eli, I've sat and watched your lips
Move without sounding.
But I know your prayerful song.
I know your dirge too deep for words,
Welling up from that ancient will to be known.
You sing, "If only you will look on your servant,
remember me, and do not forget me…"
I know your sad, silent song.
not because I read your lips,
But because my heart breaks for you to feel known.
But I also know, because I've heard this song sung before.
It has been sung by the Ishshah before you,
Named Elizabeth Cady Stanton, Harriet Tubman,
Susan B. and Rosa.
And the Ishshah before them,
Named Mary and Elisabeth, Ruth and Rachel,
Hagar and Sarah.
It is the steadfast yearning to be known,
To be remembered and so, to live.

Hannah sang this song too deep for words,
Unlock this life, and let me live.
Like Eli, I did not hear Hannah's prayer.
But I heard her song.

I want you to hear it, too,
    And know that you are known.
It is a song of healing,
    And you will thrive.
It is a song of life,
    And you will live.
It is a song of hope,
    And you will be.
It is a song of joy,
    And you will laugh.

It is a song of power,
    And you will stand.
It is a song of nurture,
    And you will feast.

This is the song sung by the Ishshah before you.
And in a little while their words will meet your lips,
    And it will be your song.
And you will rise, and you will run,
And you will smile, and you will bloom.

And I will sit down and weep,
    And give thanks that now you know,
    That you were never unknown,
    Because you are,

And your song was heard.

LOVE YOUR ENEMY

(or *The Prosthesis*)

I even more now comprehend
Loving my enemy as my friend.
I cannot hate my enemy,
I only grieve, for they are a part of me.
I learned this from the Carpenter's Son,
The Prince of Peace, whose will be done.
Non-violent, Life giving Trinity,
Tolstoy, Thoreau, King, Gandhi.
I cannot hate my enemy,
My enemy's enemy is me.
Our life is intertwined, you see,
We must love if we want to be.

But watching you I saw something more,
Than loving the one on the other shore.
For you have grieved your enemy,
The one that would have you cease to be.
Your grief is no internalization,
Dependency, or fear of isolation.
Your scans reveal that this is true
Your enemy is part of you.

You were knit together in the womb,
Tissues and organs as if on a loom.
And since the Breath of Life inspired
This bone has carried you untired.
Across the years it bore the strain
A steadfast member of your frame,

Until the day you felt the pain,
That came in waves like sheets of rain,
A sharpness like a lightning bolt,
Your loyal one began its revolt.
What once had held you straight and strong
Now a harbinger of something wrong.

Prognostic indicators showed
Healing down a narrow road.
Some art, some protocol could cure,
But there is one quick thing for sure,
The bone must go, they're all agreed,
The shortest route to victory.
Counts are good, no need to wait
A surgical strike, don't hesitate.
They nod, prepare to fire at will.
But you, you tarried, pensive and still.

"The path is clear," you said, "I agree.
But this warring flesh in your sights is me.
10 months its traitorous plot unfolded.
But 37 years since I was molded.
I was wonderfully made, whole and good.
This one just fell from whence it should.
I could not love my body less
Whether it curse or whether it bless.
So while you all praise this violent intervention,
I see the death of my flesh - and yearn for redemption."

Miriam sang while Pharaoh's men were drowning.
But YHWH said, "Silence, my children are dying."
While killing your enemy seems a necessary goal,
Wisdom sees the failure to make creation whole.
I'm sure one day I, too, will praise this reprieve,
But today, have mercy, let me grieve.
Shut your mouth, and grasp humility.
For tomorrow I say goodbye to a part of me.

Grace

I'm not mad at God.
I'm only mad for you
At the capricious chance
That a bone could betray
Embodied virtue such as yours.
So that even as you lie in hope,
You are in pain on this bed,
And I know that my touch might give joy,
But it will not release.
And perhaps it is the result of my tears,
But for the first time,
I am struggling to see Grace
In the breaking of your beautiful nature.
Then you clear your dry throat,
And inhale to buffer a wave of pain,
And you speak,
With thankful eyes, saying,
"When you left me in pre-op, I cried.
The nurse came to comfort me,
But I told her,
'I do not weep for me, for I will simply sleep.
My tears are for him,
Because he has to wait.'
Thank you for waiting for me."
And with that you reveal to me,
With perfect clarity,
The awful wonder of Grace.

Anesthesia

(or *the Surgery)*

Renée thought
        We are because we think.
Immanuel thought
        Our sense is but a prelude.
Arthur and George and Jean all thought a version of the same.
But I wonder what it ***feels*** like to think that?
And there is the irony.
Are we forms or feelings?
"Yes" is the only sensible answer.
Sensible
For to feel is our glory, said the Priest and Poet.
We know,
But we are no angels
        Who think without feeling,
        Who think without joy,
        Who think without pain.

I know you,
    Because I feel you
Because when you breathe I feel your peace,
    Because when they called
    To tell me the violence had begun,
    I felt pain in my leg,
    And joy in my heart.
And there is the blessed irony.
For to feel is to know.
Too many won't feel, so they'll never know.

And so they'll never heal from the wound
Of their desire to know.
I grieve for them.

I rejoice for you.
Because today you don't know,
Because today you won't feel
The painful irony of hurting to heal;
The irony of excising to make whole.
From the poppy fields to your sweet heart
A narcotic peace takes you from me,
Takes you from you.
Are you still you if you don't feel?
And if you can't feel, how can you heal?
I don't know,
But whether we feel or deny ourselves,
To heal is His glory.
Whence dawns my joy on this sad day when you
dare not feel.

But tomorrow you'll feel,
And that will make you sad,
And that will bring us joy.
And that is the irony.
Because you will feel, you will heal.
And that is your glory.

The Hawk

At breakfast time,
We talked with warm whispers
Of the treatment,
    The counts,
        The burns,
            The hopes,
                The boys,
            The loss,
        The laughs,
    The love.

And over my shoulder she saw you.
A flash through the window,
The feathery flurry
Of the hawk who stopped by.
You brought joy to her face,
A smile to her parched lips,
Knowing she had been graced
With the company of a rare companion.

After helping her to bed, I wondered,
If I returned the visit,
To say thank you for your thoughtful pause,
Would you come to receive my gratitude?

And so I walked barefoot,
To the edge of the wood,
And sat still,
With my heart open and my mouth closed

So that I could say, thank you
For making her smile.

After some time you came,
And alit on the magnolia at my side.
The squirrel nervously chattered,
but I smiled,
Because I knew why you had come.

So I blessed you.
        And we sat
                In silent solidarity.
                        Communion.
                She healed.
        I breathed.
You flew.

Holy other, Wholly other

The Holy Other
Knit us together.
Hope, joy, flesh, vision, will.
A union so strong it beget life,
And grace enough to share.
But one day we learned there was another
That made itself a part of you.
It's a violent way to prove the point
That while I breathe you mystically,
You are and always have been
A Wholly Other.
And it is not the translucence of a thin place
That reveals the lonely silhouette of you to me,
But the painful weight of knowing
That you must bear this Other alone.
Is a union weakened by the heartache of knowing
    That you are a Wholly Other,
    And that there is nothing I can do
    To bear this for you?
    That the limit of my solidarity
    Is the point at which I can't bear this with you?
Now I wait in the shadow of gleaning
How the Holy Other felt
Watching his Beloved suffer
As a Wholly Other.
But with you, my beloved, my Wholly Other,
This other does not threaten our union

Because of our Holy Other.
We breathe one peace,
That you, my Wholly Other, are not alone,
Because you are full of the Holy Other.
So we remain always one,
Knit together
By the Wholly, Holy Other.

Too deep for words

My hands rest on you,
Lips open to pray healing,
Only sighs will come.

HEALING

From here to forever, we'll never say
That you will be cured, only ever clean.
We must know healing in another way.
If not a future place, what can it mean?

Is healing like Peace?
The Drum Major knew Peace is no destination,
Nor can it be sustained from the outside.
It's our Soul Force, the mark of Creation,
The Way from the place where Wisdom resides.

Is healing like Freedom?
Madiba knew they can't grant your freedom.
Their will-to-power can deny dignity,
But you were made free by another kingdom.
Nothing dissuades that conscious reality.

Yes, healing must be like them.
Healing doesn't need to loosen the chains.
Pain is no power of an earthly hell.
In the Maker's eyes, your dignity's unchanged.
You are healing, at Peace, Free. You are well.

Yellow

Yellow,
The color of your ribbon,
And the label on the chemotherapy given.

Yellow,
Your bracelet urging caution to prevent,
The stars that quantify the covenant.

Yellow,
The color of a fall,
The cautionary tableau on that white wall.

Yellow,
The lemon whose oil fills my palm,
The fragrant massage of a healing balm.

Yellow,
The glow of these soft early hours,
The whimsical hue of Meredith's flowers.

Yellow,
The spire of the Chapel in the setting sun,
A reflection of hope when our day is done
And when I lay my hands on you to visualize
The Breath of Life it is no surprise
What flows through every tissue and place
It is Yellow that fills interstitial space.

Yellow,

The color of healing I've learned,
The light that holds and gently burns.
From your lungs through your body it radiates.
Chasing darkness, protective illuminate.

Yellow,

Gives me mysterious comfort that when I close my eyes,
The Healer will through this night abide.

Yellow,

A holy breath that continues to make,
The dove that will re-create.

Yellow,

The warmth that will restore you tomorrow.
The dawn of joy that melts a night of sorrow.

Yellow,

Resonates Peace like the notes on a staff.
I hear the sound of Yellow when you laugh.

Rhythm of Life

I've heard this familiar rhythm before,
As African women grind millet at dawn,
Waves crash upon the Outer Banks' shore.
Oars stroking flat boats down the Amazon.

I heard it piped in the bonnie Highlands,
Frapped on Goree's Drums that won't be enslaved,
Sung in the Sepulcher where nails pierced hands,
Chanted from the Negev's Bedouin caves.

I yearn for this rhythm of life to appear
In this clinical room this restless night.
But disjointed pulses are all that I hear.
IV pumps and buzzing fluorescent lights.

Then I hear you breathe, at peace in your sleep.
And my soul hears again that life giving beat.

Good Morning Sonnet

What used to happen to make morning good?
The sun streaming through the coconut tree.
Listening to the weaver sing to her brood.
Your head on the pillow so close to me.

Thanksgiving for life à Dieu en français.
Angels' breath blows through the net like cool bliss.
Inspiring dry bones. Proclaim life today!
Our morning prayer begun with a kiss.

But these mornings, I must give you a shot.
Beauty thus veiled in medical exile.
Where my first task is to prevent blood clots.
Yet my heart still knows beauty in this while.

Cause in our tired gaze new love is revealed.
Morning is good, for in this you are healed.

Firefly

You are finally resting.
The day was hard,
You were strong.
It hurt and you hurt.
We prayed, and in the stillness,
Grace found you.
So now you sleep.
Ushered in by 10 milligrams,
perhaps.

But now, it doesn't matter.
You sleep, and I am filled with gratitude.
So here I sit, in the candle lit corner.
Heart to hand,
Hand to pen,
Pen to notebook,
Recording my joy for you
In these silent words,
Because to speak them aloud
Would be to shatter their muse.

So, my muted gratitude seems to return to me,
Unshared, unheard, unknown.
Perhaps that is the definition of lonely.
Then, through the night blackened pane of glass,
I see a firefly.

With every breath,
He reflects his gratitude to the world.
He radiates his joy the only way he can.
Brilliant, yet, in silence, unheard, unknown.
Perhaps he's feeling lonely, too.
But he is not.
Because I perceive his pulse of joy.
I see what he shared with me this night.
He is not alone.
And neither am I.
Linger with me a little longer, firefly,
And see how graciously sleep has found her.
Can you see my joy?

Thank you for sharing yours.

While you were home healing

I missed you today.

We three tried to enjoy it.

But you felt so far.

Always the Mountain

We've returned to the gorge,
This valley where I was formed in my youth,
To convalesce along her web of trails
That usher us between old friends.
I find peace in looking up
To the ridge that circumscribes my way,
Because I know where I am
As long as I can see who stands sentinel to my right.
Table, Bearback, Hawksbill, Grandfather and Sugar,
A communion of saints circled about me
And I know I have returned to the healing place.

I am returned to my old friends:
The damp smell of mountain laurel
        That clots the gash
        Cut by the falling stream,
The green moss that silences my footfall,
The white lichen on the burning beech,
        Set a blaze by the autumnal rays of a southern sun,
The yellow glow of this sweet maple corridor
        Through which I and the chipmunk run,
The spider's lace bejeweled in dew,
The salty kiss of this cave
        And her stalactites that guard the going out and the coming in
        Of the first nations
        And now me.
The wild turkeys on our ascent,
The trout below her cold falls,

The hawk, the deer,
The wolf, the bear,
The wooly worm on the wild strawberry,
The flowers and fruits of this mountain
    That inspire the taste of her jam and honey.
I am sustained by the mutual conversation and consolation
    Of life on this mountain
    that reminds me
On this mountain you made us,
and by this mountain you heal us.
Or maybe it is the voice of the mountain itself,
    Whose minerals, formed before man ever joined in
    reply,
    Are now exposed by the laurels roots.
I feel the ore's magnetic call
    and sense the rock's salty speech
    Telling a truth so deep,
    Emerging now from below
    where creation continues as it was in the beginning.
The rocks' very being
Now a prophetic speech act that,
    after violent making by force or fissure,
    Peace will endure
    For the eons that rest,
    As a sign of healing,
    A sure and certain hope that now begets new life,
    And into this valley the cup of life keeps running over.

To this abundant feast of life
I have brought my beloved.

And now I sit with her,
Warm cup in one hand and hers in the other,
Listening to this mountain wake up,
Communicating from eternity,
Once more filling this valley with your truth
    That surely goodness and mercy will follow her all the days of her life.
And I am at peace again
Knowing that you are healing her
On your holy mountain.

Good News

(or ***The Sublime***)

I never had quite understood
The meaning of the word Sublime.
It seemed to me if something's good,
How could it cause dread in your mind?

I do know well how goodness
Can stand righteously indignant
Among those things that cause distress,
From disease and threat emergent.

Proclaiming, "I am hope and life.
You can pollute and violate,
Corrupt, exploit, and wage strife,
Sow your fear and cultivate hate,

And yet I am here, look to me!
In my love, there's no room for fear,
I'm the only reality."
Beauty is the face goodness wears.

True, but Immanuel once said,
There's goodness of another kind,
That can fill you with holy dread.
Awesomeness. That is the sublime.

Not the awe of wealth, fame or kings
That dazzles with contrived beauty,
While only emptiness they bring,
With their meaningless calories,

But awe in the presence of real,
Native beauty of a creature
That compels my soul to revere,
Arrested by some felt feature,

That resounds haunting holiness,
Resonating through this thin place.
The heart is provoked to express
Awe to see Divine Beauty's face.

I cannot feel happiness here,
Driven to deeper devotion
I take off my sandals in fear
To honor this unnamed emotion.

That is the sense of the sublime,
Which knows pain conjoins the blessing
Of God mingling with us in time,
Like Jacob after his wrestling.

I embrace the gift of good news
Each clean scan a bold step for my wife.
Yet something lingers when fear's removed,
This blessing limps into our life.

This joy demands sobriety,
Your healing is made too profound
In contrast with reality
That grace and nature remain bound.

Perhaps that is the reason why,
As others giggle each good news,
I retreat into your blue eyes
And feel your thoughts in deeper hues.

My soul stands still in great respect,
Of the price your body has paid,
For it is your wrestling with death,
That has so sweet this good news made.

Today you've held chaos at bay,
But I cannot make platitudes.
This news demands another way.
This knowing provokes sheer gratitude.

So, barefoot, I homage humbly,
Hold hands, kiss your head, wipe our tears,
In awe of this sublimity,
And the holiness it reveals.

THE SIGN

A healing prayer
Is not a request to God.
It is the Rainbow.

Socks and Sliced Bread

(during your inpatient stay on the boys' first day of school)

Tomorrow, it's back to school.
We finished dinner.
I rinsed the plates.
I loaded the dishwasher.
I picked up the towels from the bathroom floor.
I collected their socks,
Put their shoes by the door.
I counted out bread slices.
Turkey and cheese.
Carrots and berries.
Seeds and yogurt.
I zipped the lunch boxes.
I wiped down the counter.
I helped pack school bags,
Signed agendas,
Binders, books and pens.

I hugged them, I kissed them.
I held them a little longer,
Because they wouldn't let go,
Because you weren't here,
Because you were there.

I wiped their tears.
I wiped mine.
I tucked them in.

"Je vous aime."
"I miss her, too."
"I know it's hard, but try to sleep."
Tomorrow's a new day,
Back to school.

Radiation

Breath.
Breathe in…reconcile.
Breathe out…create.

Radiation.
Radiate into…annihilate.
Radiate out…illuminate.

Radiation into.
Radiation streaming into you.
Beams of energy vibrating through,
Searing tissue to designated depths.
Delivering pulses of targeted death.
You absorb that white hot heat,
Without seeing or feeling its entry,
Willing to be violated,
Knowing the path to healing must be radiated.

Breathe in.
You are shot through with manufactured energy,
Purpose built to annihilate,
Gladly trading tumors for blisters,
This radiation decimates.

Breathe out.
You are shot through with Divine energy,
Lovingly crafted to animate,
Daily inspiring your carbon to life,
This radiation illuminates.

Radiate out.
You emit a holy, yellow warmth,
Desiring to return this peace,
Wanting to illuminate
The grace filled path to wholeness.

Radiation streaming out of you.
Source of energy flowing through,
Reconciling hope from unknown heights.
You're a radiant plenitude of created life.

The Monarch

I am standing, waist in the waves
Facing Senegal where this tide is running.
I am rejoicing in the squeals of my two boys,
And the tug of their hands
Finding anchor in my arms against the salty pull of this vaguery,
When over my shoulder he flutters.
And I'm wondering,
Why would this Monarch leave his dominion of sea oats and dunes
To skim these rough waves
Towards a continent that he cannot see?
So I watched it fly,
Southeast as far as my eye could follow him,
This paper thin force of nature,
Flying between Cancer and Capricorn
As black and orange have flown from age to age,
Without fear of the danger boiling below,
Only flying because by nature he has been transformed.

Then I look back over my shoulder,
And from the waves I see you,
Sitting on the deck of the dune whence the Monarch came.
You smile and wave at us.
Your gestures of joy, like your yellow hat, fluttering in the wind
Towards a future that we cannot see.
You are a gentle force of nature
Flying between Cancer and hope,

As life has flown from age to age,
Without fear of any danger boiling below,
Only flying because by grace you have been transformed.

So as I stand, waist in the waves,
Holding on to our two boys
Seeking anchor in this rough sea
    somewhere between Senegal and this shore,
We watch you fly,
And rejoicing in your renaissance, we take wing.

The Proper Art of Healing

Diagnosing is a science,
But healing is an art.
We must observe to judge the measure of your foe.
But there is no protocol
That can set the parameters
Of the path you must take.
No, the proper work of healing
Is to return to you.
Not content to observe,
Nor intent to tell you where or how,
We can only attend to you.
To attend is to wait,
    To hear,
    To receive,
    To seek to understand,
    To listen to what you know
Of when it is time,
And where you must go.
For your healing, like your disease,
Is uniquely yours.

They can say, "I've seen",
But they won't.
They can say "I know",
But they don't.
They can say, "Because",
But they can't feel the effect.

It may be true that there are others
Who have walked through this bone strewn valley,
But they have not trodden this dirt with your feet,
on your swollen knee,
Breathed through your lungs,
Powered by your pulse,
Seen through the eyes of your heart,
And felt your body in this painscape
Feeling its way by faith,
The path to the banquet.
But you are learning the way.
And you are learning the steps,
And you are learning when to take them.
And you welcome the poison with patience.
You bless the burning as part of your radiant redemption.
You allow the surgical strike and solitary steps
As partners who are necessary, but never sufficient.
They must leave room on this journey,
For the art of healing,
For the fruits of the earth on your palette,
For restoring oils on your skin,
For the beauty of art in your eyes,
For the Word of Life in your ears,
For the scent of sea salt in your nose,
For love's embrace inside of you,
For in all of this lies the mystery of healing.
Because you are no machine,
And you do not survive.
You are alive, and you heal.

So I wait.

I listen.
I follow.
I attend.
While you have called me to join you on this path,
You are the artisan.

She Walks

If I need to remember, I walk.
When I've been abroad for far too long,
Bracketed by asphalt and rubber,
Conditioned air and gas and glass,
Tempted to frame my view with popular frenzy manufactured on airwaves,
I walk.
And I remember.
I return home to listen
To the goose, the deer, the box turtle,
The honeysuckle, the dragonfly,
The creek, the wind, the child,
The rock and the raccoon,
The snake and the tree,
Who remind me who I am.

If you want to see how well a people know who they are,
Watch how much they walk.
Paul walked the Areopagus
to learn who the Athenians were.
Buddha walked beyond the palace walls
to know whence came truth.
Keats, Thoreau, Blake and Frost all walked in the woods
To figure the world in a flower and gratitude in a blade of grass.
Muir walked the Sierra Nevada
to find his thread woven into creation's tapestry
Gandhi walked to the sea
to taste the saltiness of justice.

King walked in the light of day

    so that our consciousness would be illuminated by
    Blackness.

They walked, and they remembered who we are.

And we have sojourned ensemble,
A promenade of love,
Hand in hand and foot to path.
Along the canals of Copenhagen,
    On the sands of Skagen,
    Over Rome's seven hills,
    Into the patisseries of Paris,
    Through the contemplative traverses of Taize,
    Up the towers of Tallinn,
    Down the alleys of Amsterdam,
    To the temples of Turkey,
    In the barcas of Barbados,
    And under the Senegalese Sun
    You and I have bloomed
    By sharing this unmediated way of knowing.
We have loved
because we walked,
and the world reminded us who we are.
And this truth has set us free,
To be.

But this has been for you a season of bondage.
A tumorous winter, when pain confined you in these walls.
It tried to convince you of fear and loss,
    By multiplying distances to unreachable lengths,
    By dividing time into painfully unending seconds,
    By denying you access to the truth,

to the goose and the river, the bush and the wind,
who never stopped calling in rhythm,
come, hear, feel and know,
Remember, my sister, remember!

So that is why, beloved, we rejoice.
Because the icy pain that froze your feet
Has thawed into the Spring of Life.
Not a new life, rather, a remembering.
Because, once desiccated by pain and poison and cold steel,
Your sinews felt that breath of life,
And knit themselves into a spring of motion.
They remember how to pulse and pull,
How to rise and push, one step, then two.
And now, in the warmth of the Spring of this Breath,
They remember who you are,
and you rise,
and you walk.
And we cry,
Knowing now that you are free.
Not free from fear or loss or pain,
But free to return
To knowing yourself,
Because now you walk.
Now you can return to the deer, the child,
The wind, the box turtle, the truth.
Now you hear.
Now you feel.
Now you know
Now you remember.
So now you heal.

TA BEAUTÉ

C'est difficile d'être ici sans toi.
Je me souviens qu'ici, c'est si jolie.
Mais, quand je suis revenu,
Tu n'étais pas là.
Et ce lieu n'est pas si jolie,
Sans ta beauté.

Hard to be Light Hearted

Joy, Sorrow, Melancholy, Happiness,
Ecstasy, Anger, Hilarity, Fear,
Surprise, Compassion, Wonder, Tenderness,
My heart has held each throughout the years.

Yet my heart always stayed unchanged despite
The weight of emotions that filled its rooms
Life's Pleasures and Pains rendered my heart light,
Like a wing that knows drag helps it take flight.

But this Noel your heart receives a gift
Deep in the recesses of its chambers,
Whose gravity alters the physics of lift
And seems to tether my heart to the earth.

It's strange. That which caused me to laugh in life
Seem like vapid, vacuous distractions,
and my silence makes them all wonder, Why
I'm now muted by some unseen burden?

I want to answer them and explain how
My laughter and mirth have not departed.
I've just learned to sound true depths of joy now,
So profound it's hard to be light hearted.

So I wait the Angels' news of Peace that once more
Will make our hearts light and once again soar.

The return to Hann Mariste

Why is it so hard to be here in this place?

Because places are more than spaces.
They aren't a vacuum
In which life happened.
They are a place
That helped give meaning to a moment;
Color to a vision;
Texture to a feeling;
Scent to a smell;
Flavor to a taste.

This place is a vessel
That holds a spirit
That remains long after you've gone.
Like the heat that rests in my skin
When your hand leaves mine.
Your warmth,
Your energy,
Your sweat,
Your essence,
They are now a part of me,
Because we held each other.

And so it is with this place.

Because it held us.

In its embrace we laughed,

We dreamed,

We smiled,

We slept,

We cried,

We ate,

We learned,

We grew,

We hosted,

We prayed,

We fell ill,

We healed,

We drank,

We talked,

We listened,

We played,

We loved,

We lived.

That's why it hurts to be here.

Because you are here.

Yet you are not.

Bluebird

Autumn.
It's not fall.
It's a falling.
A slow release of each strand
Returning to the earth.
It may be beautiful,
But there is a quiet anguish
In this flirtation with death.
Being able to see through bare limbs
To parts normally adorned
With shocks of blonde, brown and red.
I can now see through you to what lies beyond.
This shorn stillness makes you seem vulnerable,
As if the earth is wicking the sap from each blooming place.
And even though I am resting beside you,
Watching this falling makes me feel alone,
As if I am cursed to witness a beautiful thing fade.
But your barrenness affords me a new blessing.
Because the unadorned state of your branches reveals the
bluebird.
And every flick of his indigo feathers
Shows a beating red breast beneath.
And I am recalled to the mystery
That autumn is not a sacrifice of beauty for loss.
It is a conservation that nurtures
the bud of new life.

Now revived
by the repose of this sight,
I can breathe again
Knowing that, resting somewhere
within your bare branches,
The bluebird sings.
And I can wait
for your Spring.

A Star in the West

When the setting sun

Turned December clouds purple,

Venus calmed my heart.

Being or Becoming?

(or *Advent*)

Temptation is yearning to become
Something other than what you are.
To have, hold, or be something other
To take up more or less time
That you determine to be fair.
To live beyond the weight and space
Of what you conserve or return in thanks.
To consume what was bequeathed
By creation's communion of saints
Without even realizing
"Thou art the man", the great ancestor
of those who are yet to be knit
Of carbon, spirit and stardust,
And yet already pray aloud
That you will always be content,
Not tempted to become other
That the fruition of what you are.

I've seen an ape share her orange
I've never seen a dolphin
Try to fly or nest in a tree.
I don't believe their mean estate
Is due to any kind of lack
Of hope or imagination.
No, it's just that this moral state

Is the mark of our peculiar race.
We who ignore the tree of life,
To eat sweet fruit of a tree
of knowledge of good and evil
We trade our birthright,
the healing of nations,
to try and become
Something we fashion as God.

In this, yes, Heidegger was right
To shine light on the cave's shadows.
If the Holy is found in being,
Then becoming is our temptation.

Revealed, now, is the source of my strife
I know I court temptation
Asking stone to be turned to bread
To avoid this particular fast.
But I demand that she become,
Cause I know that deep in your heart
You, too, want your daughter to be healed.

No, I know you see the sparrow
And though she falls, she is still loved,
And returns to dust to nourish the rose.
So she is, and so will I.
And I love so completely
All her scars and pain and fatigue
That I could never dream of more

Than the beauty that she is now.
And so I bathe in gratitude
And listen to the lovely song
Of my sparrow this blessed morn,
And I will return all my thanks
For the being that she is, full stop.
But I fear that's where my faith ends,
For I am a son of Adam.
And I will claim my sin boldly
Because I believe more boldly.
So I will tempt you like Jairus.
I dare to answer your question,
"Tell me, what do you want from me?"
Son of David, visit this night.
Maranatha.
Breathe over her, alight.
No, in the end, I don't think I have sinned.
I only ask for your advent.
Because I don't ask for her becoming
To spite what you made her to be.
Her being was meant to flourish.
The second Adam returned
To restore us to what we are.

So by healing, I do not demand
She become something other than she.
I ask only that you return.
Let her flower. Let her be.

There will be Love

Standing at a threshold
Of an hour that tells me
I must cross into a new age.
While everyone falls in
With a kiss and a laugh,
I step with a firm stride
That knows the charade.
Because the reality
Is that this particular hour
Is no more significant,
Bears no more hope,
Holds no more promise
Than this time yesterday,
Or the new tomorrow
Into which this eve leans.
And that is why I never cared
So much to sing Burns' Ode
And sanctify this heathen hour
Above the one that God has given me.
Saint Peter knew
What Einstein proved
That there is no important hour
Except the one that you feel.
For time is not what passes,
Time is not what pushes,
Time is not what brings.

Time is nothing more
Than your experience of the real
Inbreaking of life
In its eternal fullness.
Time is only the measure
Of your movement
Into the moment when you realize
Incarnate presence.
Time is a moment of grace
For in it, you know
You are alive to feel it.

So standing at this threshold,
I do not blaspheme
And ask what a new year will bring.
For a new year brings nothing.
I will not feel the passing of time.
I will only feel the wonder of grace
In each holy moment that will be.
I dare not wish, need not resolve,
Because I already know
The mystery that will be.
For there will be Love.
There will be tears,
And laughter that will dry them,
And in it all
There will be Love.

There will be pain
And there will be anesthetics
And when senses dull
There will be Love.

There will be dreams
And we will realize
And when we reach the limit of faith
There will be Love.

We will strive to our End
And we will arrive
And when hope has no place,
There will be Love.
There will be desire
And we will unite,
And when exhausted we fall
There will be Love.

There will be sunsets
And there will be dawns,
And whether we hold vigil or sleep,
There will be Love.
There will be singing
And meals
And photos
And fears
And sickness

And games

And prayers

And holding hands

And work

And chemo

And losses

And gains

And in the theater between them all and you and me,

There will be Love.

And that is why

Standing at this threshold,

I do not fear or want for the passing of time

Because there will be nothing new

That the stars have not already seen.

For even now, with my hand in yours,

There is Love.

Emmanuel.

So, this hour is no passing of time.

This is the fullness of time.

This is the presence of eternity incarnate.

This is Love.

Sandalwood

Sandalwood's sweet smoke
Is the fragrance of my care,
My rising prayer.

What the Child Knows

When he picked up that little child
And set her in the center,
We rejoiced and ran off to proclaim
That now we know.
We know the answer to power
Is to overcome it with another kind.
A childlike power will win us our kingdom!
But when we ran off to teach
What we thought we had learned,
We left behind a man named Jesus,
Who held a little child on his knee.
Not a soul stayed to ask
What the child knows.

What the child knows
Is that the kind man from Nazareth
Was not teaching some new kind of power.
He was not teaching us a new way to rule our kingdom.
He was helping a child to know
    What it felt like to be seen
    What it felt like to be held
    What it felt like to be loved
    What it felt like to be dignified
    What it felt like to be known.
But we wouldn't know, now would we?
Because we run off too quickly.

We read too fast, and never stop to ask,
Who was that child?

Funny isn't it?
The very child that Jesus held,
Saying, if you want to live
Be like this one.
We are so enamored with our cultured knowing
We never even care to ask,
"Which one?"
"Who is this hero of mine?"
"What does this child know?"

My child,
I've walked you through this life,
To the plane, the palace, the car, the bus,
The school, the castle, the embassy,
The mountain, the church, the river,
Across Copenhagen,
France, London, Dakar,
And I've tried to listen
To your answer when I ask
"What do you know, child?"
I resist running off too quickly to proclaim
"Look here," "Taste that," "See this,"
"Speak so," "Think this for thus sayeth the Lord!"
No, I have tried to stay near
Quietly beside you,

Watching

how you see Mona Lisa's smirk and wonder,

how you follow the curves of Venus de Milo and

blush,

how you feel the cold stone of Notre Dame and pray,

how you hear Mozart in the Schönbrunn and dance,

how you peer into the tea colored Loch Ness and imagine,

how you listen to the call resound across the Sahara and pause,

how you kneel at the rail and take hold of His body.

So that I might know when to ask,

"What did He say to you?"

"What did you learn from Him, my child?"

Now in these days

I lead you by the hand,

Through these halls,

To therapy and treatment,

To the cafeteria and the consult room,

To a chair in the waiting room,

To the toys in your cousins' room

To the bed in grandma's house,

To a new school,

To the stranger-new friend's party.

In this strangely dislodged life

Among these people who have just fled His presence,

Proclaiming the gospel of whatever they think they heard.

New prophets of protocol and pop psychology
Who want to distract you, telling you,
"Eat ice cream, child, and smile"
"Don't worry, child, they are smart,"
"He is good and she is strong."

But they have not tried to sit on her weak knee
Like you have.
And they have not heard what He has said to you in your prayers,
In your quiet heart,
When the crowds leave,
And you see her strain to stand,
And reach out to hold you,
And awake too early to pray with us,
And cry over the beauty of your art,
And defy fatigue to listen to you read,
And cuddle you despite the cords,
And show you that life is now,
And hope doesn't wait for a cure,
And faith doesn't require results,
And peace doesn't need tranquility
And healing doesn't depend on death's decisions,
And having a new power to overcome power isn't the point.

But I see you,

And I hold you,

And I love you,

And so, my child,

I want to know what all this means from your place in the circle?

Tell me, child,

While we all turned away to talk at each other,

What did the nice man from Nazareth tell you?

Because that is what I need to learn.

Twister

We often measured
This season's passage
By what you have lost:
A full night of sleep.
Rising from a chair
    without steadying.
Being quite able
    to plan a future
    without qualification.
Enjoying moments
    without feeling need
    to frame each second
    of your children's smiles.
Energy to wait
    35 minutes
    for the next table.
Your job and our home.
First world luxury
    of feigning interest
    in popular trends
    masquerading as
    some kind of culture
    so as not to offend
    the near-sighted ones.
Spontaneous sex.

The immunity

to care for the sick.

Shame to ask for help.

All prejudices

about those in need

who yearn, but can't do.

Fear of reaching out.

Procrastination.

Timid modesty.

Categorical

imperative thoughts.

Your capacity

to stand long enough

to prepare a meal

without pause to rest.

Needing to buy shampoo.

Our dancing lessons.

Feeling well at least

three out of four weeks.

Hiking these mountains.

Sitting in full Sun.

The use of your leg.

The ability

in a crowd, to be

inconspicuous.

Naïve youthfulness

of overlooking

a pain or sore spot.

Comforting your child
　　on your right knee, or
　　while you're inpatient.
Freedom to order
　　food without thinking
　　about mouth blisters.
A year's vocation.
Kneeling to receive
　　the reconciling
　　Sacrament of grace.
Teaching them to ski
Teacher conferences.
Driving them to school.
Short-term memory.
Your full person-hood
　　in onlooker's eyes.
A certain degree
　　of your agency
　　to accommodate
　　all of those keeners
　　who think they're helping,
　　but who are really
　　taking roles from you
　　that you must fulfill
　　to feel you have saved
　　your identity
　　from the gravity
　　of this black matter.

Blissful ignorance
    of your white blood counts,
    of your neutrophils
    of your temperature
    hour by hour.
Hugs from friends abroad.
Light hearted hours
    without interruption
    from the nausea
    or from hot flashes,
    or from the fatigue,
    a sublime dread, or
    an ecstatic hope.
These are the many things,
    among many more
    of the native fruits
    in your life's garden
    that cancer has spoiled.
But on Christmas Day
    I did discover
    another real loss.
Our son anxiously
    unwrapped his present.
He was filled with joy,
    but I realized
    immediately
    you can't play Twister.

You can no longer

    put your right foot green

    and left foot yellow

    to be the winner.

But he needn't grieve.

You can be the spinner.

Yaangi fi

Maangi fi.

Est-ce que ça suffit?

It seemed to me

as strangely,

this way to greet a life,

to seek to know

little more than,

"I am here."

Shouldn't we yearn

to marvel at more,

of heights and lengths to come?

If you had asked

fifteen years ago,

"What marvels do you dream?"

I would have told you textured tales

of far away lands and languages

of palaces and planes,

of seas and fjords,

and old world charm,

of mermaids and tin soldiers,

bagpipes and heather,

castles and caleidhs,

of sensual soirées in the east of France,

and coffee in the ruined suqs of Turkey

or the seven hills of Rome,

of our children's laughter,

at home beneath

a Saltire or Dannebrog,

or the crackling shade of a coco-palm,

around a bowl,

sipping jus de gingembre

by painted pirogues.

But now that we

Have tasted and seen,

more vivid than a dream,

and warmed our souls

by the fire that burns,

and the tree that blooms

at the centre of it all,

If you ask me now, to visualize

which enchantment

do I most prize?

I close my eyes,

and my soul sees,

not Coliseums,

or Royal Miles,

or Parisienne Parks

or Baltic beaches,

But that I was blessed
to be at your side.

Only there, just to be,
transforming me to we,
revealing love's deep mystery,
that all we seek
from life I see.
Ça suffit,
ma cherie,
to know simply,
Yaangi fi.

Twelfth Night

And so it was
In Elizabeth's time
On the Twelfth Night of Christmastide.
The last night to fête
The feast of an Incarnation.
Music, a dance,
A song, a drama
A penultimate moment
To embody a blessing
In one final gift.

Ours is no Tudor ball
Or Shakespearian tale.
But we sit in this theater,
On the Twelfth Night,
Awaiting an image
Of magnetic truth
That will reveal
The state of healing
That has become
Incarnate in her flesh.

And so it is
That we pray
On this Twelfth Night of Christmastide
With the hosts of heaven.
Peace on earth
And in this queen of creation.

Spirit of Life,
Who embodied Peace on the First Night,
There is still time to incarnate,
To reveal one more gift
On this Twelfth Night.
Let it be so.

Dust

(or ***Ash Wednesday***)

Now Remember
That you are dust
And back to earth
To dust you must.

They walk around
With ashen trace
Lamenting now
Encountered fate.

Dark prolepsis
Of what will be
Recalls life is
Fragmentary.

Reminded we
Struggle to face
Humility
Knowing our place

That seems to be
Hard for our race
But not for me.
Dust I embrace.

For all along
Earth's ashen lace
I hear life's song
In every place.

In death, in birth,
In our union,
A holy breath,
Deep communion.

Expiration
The stuff of one,
Inspiration
The chain links on.

My end is not
a fragmentation
My instance is
Participation.

I've never come
This way before,
But my own flesh
Is life's encore.

The wolf, the slug,
The peat and me,
Share a star's dust
Collectively.

Ejected by
God's will to love
Each ashen life
His goodness proves.

This water drop
That nurtures me
Once rode a comet
That filled the sea,

That grew the tree
That made the fruit,
The bird would feed
The serpent's need,

Whose corps became
Earth's energy,
A pressured vein
Released by streams

That fed the fish
That grew the corn
That fuelled love's wish
And I was born.

Enlightened by
Gaia's labyrinth,
I drink the vine,
Wisdom's absinth,

That burns then smiles
As I survey
The dusty piles
Along my way,

That took the form
Of flowers, bees,
The rotting log
In which I see

Life this Wednesday
With my child's eye
Another way
To comprehend why

When back to dust
Carbon descends
No fragmented
Grieved lament.

For life has won
You lived, laughed,
You gave, you loved,
The point is that.

Grieve not your time bound
Ashen making,
Give gratitude
For life's in breaking.

I Miss Me

On that cold January Day,
My heart broke when I heard you say,
"Of all I've lost of necessity,
Sometimes I'm sad, because I miss me."

I know it's more than physicality,
Losing innocence and agency,
But I honor when you say to me,
I want healing to restore my beauty.

Every soul needs to see beauty,
That's not ignoble vanity,
I want to live beautifully,
But what is art and what is ugly?

It's not that I don't see your scars,
And remember you the way you are,
Before the healing parched your lips,
And numbness filled your fingertips,

Bright eyes eclipsed by dark fatigue,
Muscles weakened atrophy,
A blistered throat that strains to sing
And hands too weak to stich a dream,

But you wonder from your side of the bed
Where you rest your heavy head
If I'm too bent to make or sing,
Have I lost my true beauty?

I hear the grief in what you say,
But your essence hasn't changed.
Don't say "That's just the way you see me",
I see goodness, and the truth is - that's beauty.

On Beauty

Today is grace.
But I am tired.
Because I sat vigil all night
Contemplating beauty.
At least I think I did.

I reclined there beside you
In that familiar way
When I turn out the light
After we read
Or make love
Or pray that peace will spend the night,
And wait for that hour
When angels' breath convinces your soul
That it's ok to let go and rest.

But last night
I told them no, not yet.
She's too beautiful to leave.
And hearing my plaintiff prayer,
They let me stay, I think.

And in that quiet, I heard someone come.
Schopenhauer slipped through the door.
He kneeled by my side.
Hey, Art. She's beautiful, isn't she.

"Of course she is,
This is your dream," he said.
"Everything in your dream is beautiful,
Because it's your will."

I sat up
To catch the gaze of his eyes,
To make sure he heard me when I said,
Wait, my friend,
Beauty has nothing to do with my will.
If my will be done,
There would be no fear
To exhaust her in this dream,
No pain, nor need of hope.
You prattle on about will,
But in my dreams
I still see her scars,
And parched lips,
Fatigue stained eyes,
Her blistered throat too sore to sing,
And fingertips
To numb to make something.
These sights won't let me put down her pain
In my day or in my dreams,
And yet she's brilliant
In the light of her day
Or the dark of her night.

"Tis true," said a voice
Of another standing close by.
It was Nietzsche
Who found his way in.
"Yes, we heard her
When she said she missed herself.
This season of her un-becoming
Will reveal the beauty that rests
When flesh is annihilated.
So I agree, that which breaks her down
Is a gift in the end, you see,
Which is the beauty in every tragedy."

To which I turned and said,
Too sharply I fear,
"Open your eyes, you shrew,
Take hold of someone's hand,
And come back to your senses.
I grant you,
There is an abiding unity
The mysterious energy,
But my friend,
The dissolution of the flesh is not what made the Bacchanalia beautiful!
The variety of bodies
With every blessed curve and fault
Singing in harmony,
Uniting in love,

To honor the fruit of the earth
Drunk with the Breath of the One
Who called her to life
So that she might feel pain and know joy.
They were beautiful and good.
My God, you missed the boat, Fred!
It's her imperfect incarnation
That unveils the beauty
Which you cast out
Just so you could go and find it.
But look, it is here.
Her life is good, she is beautiful,
And that's the truth!

"Too right," cheered David Hume
Who waddled into the room.
"Of course she's beautiful.
After all,
It's you who sees her with your eyes.
From all the years of youthful love,
You've developed quite the taste
For the one whose form you behold,
Which defines for you, beauty's face."

David, my friend, I paused to say,
Methinks the Haggis
And too many wee drams
Has blurred your vision

And dulled your wonder,
Which is our most important sense.
I've not suddenly discovered
That I'm attracted to baldness
Or those who are bent
And wearied with the pain of fear,
You insensitive,
Self-centered twit.
I'm talking about Beauty,
Who has nothing to do with me
And whether I prefer
A runway waif
Or a full bodied romantic.
Beauty doesn't need
My affirmation,
My inclination,
Or my affectation,
Because she's already there
Before I noticed her.
And I don't care who you are,
Buddhist or Christian,
Sikh, Muslim, or Jew,
Atheist or confused,
Gay or straight, too,
Come and see,
Watch her walk, smile and live,
Behold her shine
And the darkness fly,

And you will say,
'My God that is Beauty!'

"Well reasoned," cogitated Immanuel Kant
Whose head barely fit in the bedroom door.
"If it is to be said that she's beautiful,
Everyone must agree universally.
As you say, we would be hard pressed
To find one soul who disagreed.
But for the task of distinguishing
Whether she has native beauty
Or whether your judgment
Is subject to an aesthetic,
You neglect one fact:
You, sir, are interested for you have much to lose.
So I suggest that your judgment
Is reasoned from a perspective of fear
Of losing your love,
    Your partner, your trust,
    Your confessor, your friend,
    Your support, your lover,
    Your laughter, your muse,
    Your hand, your ear,
    Your heart, your breath,
To something truly awesome.
And that, my friend,
Is no vision of beauty,
But the rush of the sublime."

Well, Immanuel, I said,

Like everything, you are a little bit right.

I am deeply interested.

But I disagree that interested love

Is not Divine,

For interest begets relationality.

I need her love to make me better.

But that doesn't spoil my judgment,

Because Beauty is not subjective.

Beauty is not an aesthetic.

We have aesthetics because there is beauty.

A bird's song is not a prelude

To my mind's own symphony.

The bird's song is harmony incarnate.

Do I fear for my life at her loss?

Yes, but that is not

What makes me judge her beautiful.

She is the birdsong

Whether I stopped to listen or not.

I only give thanks to the Artisan

For making her sing,

And for opening the ears of my soul

That awakened the eyes of my heart

That led me to contemplate

The True Beauty of this being.

At this point, it seemed,
I was growing frustrated
From describing a rose to thorns.

So I turned away from them to her,
And then I felt a strong hand on my shoulder.

"I know it's hard to find a way
To catch a shooting star."
I recognized Plato's voice,
And gave thanks for a Greek among Romans.
We walked a lap around the room
Behind the other guests.
"Have courage,
Remember what I taught.
Beautiful things are difficult."

Immediately my heart rate fell.
I returned to my guests with grace.
I know we're all looking for the same thing,
To know Beauty's harmony resonating in our being.
We can't describe how,
Or what or why,
But Beauty revealed herself to me.

Then one by one they left.
Plato took my hand and said,
"It seems beauty has taken her form."

Nietzsche paused to admit,
"Her presence does magnify."
Hume nodded and yielded,
"It's not just you, her healing beckons us all."
Kant consoled,
"Do not fear,
For right or wrong, she remains beautiful."
Schopenhauer tapped my crown, and reassured,
"You can wake up anytime.
I feel sure that you will find
Beauty is still there,
Right beside you all the while."

So I closed the door,
Crawled back into bed,
Gave thanks for Beauty's sleep,
And held fast to the joy
Of knowing for sure
I've been blessed with Beauty's keep.

Logos

Whatever was said to Rumi,
Which was said to the rose,
Which was said to the Cyprus,
Which was said to the jasmine
And the sugarcane,
It was said to me.
Logos,
Ruha.
It is creative,
And now life is sweet.

Made in the USA
Middletown, DE
29 August 2023

37566100R00078